PLAYGROUND EDUCATION

CREATED and WRITTEN by

R. TOBIAS PITTMAN

THE EDUCATIONAL PANDA

PUGSLEY PANDA

ILLUSTRATIONS by

William Chislum

EDITED by

Gloria Miles

Playground Education and Entertainment
www.pugsleypanda.com | email: pugsleypanda@gmail.com

Hi Desmond, what are you doing?
I'm packing for my vacation. My father said we are driving through the New England States. I don't know which states are the New England States. Do you know where there're located?

We are talking about vowels in the alphabet. Can you help us recognize them?
Maybe English Ellen can help.

Hi Nutrition Nancy, Pugsley and I are on our way to the playground. Do you want to come with us?
I'm on my way to the grocery store with my mother. We're going to get some fruits and vegetables.
Fruits and vegetables are important.

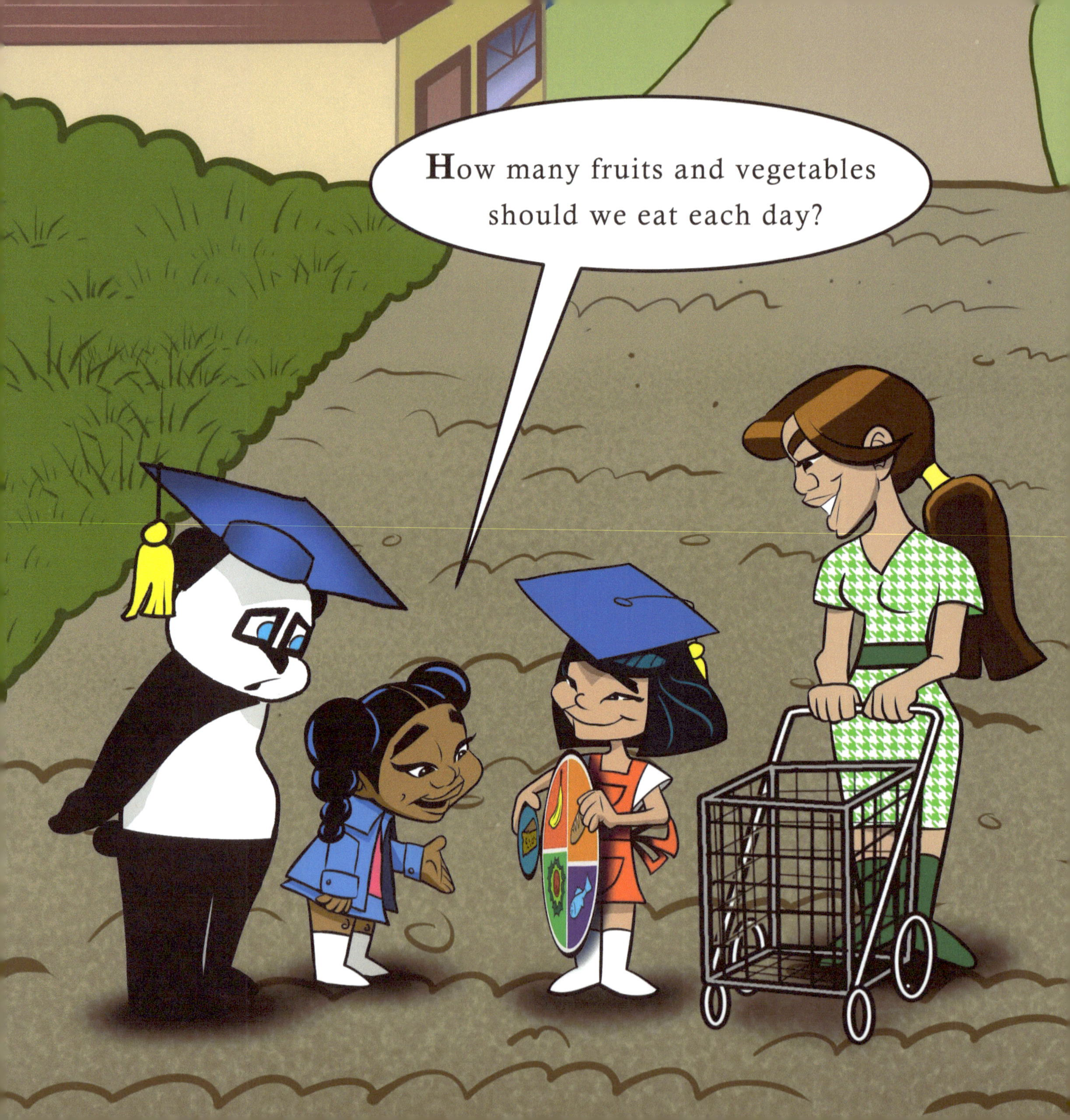
How many fruits and vegetables should we eat each day?

Since it's so hot, what should we do Safety Sam?
WELLINGTON HILL
You have to drink more water so you won't get dehydrated. Remember this: "As the temperature rises, drinking more water would be the wisest".

We had a nice walk up Wellington Hill.
Along the way we met some of the Educational Kids.
We met Geography Gerald, English Ellen,
Nutrition Nancy, Safety Sam, and Math Mary.
We finally made it to the playground
at the top of Wellington Hill.

ENJOY ALL THESE OTHER CHILDREN'S BOOKS FROM

PLAYGROUND EDUCATION

"No Bullying"
By
Safety Sam

"Wellington Hill Playground"
By
The Educational Kidz

"Famous Landmarks in The United States"
By
Geography Gerald

"Seasonal Safety Tips for Children"
By
Safety Sam

"How Does Water Recycle "
By
Science Scott

PUGSLEY PANDA

www.ingramcontent.com/pod-product-compliance
Lightning Source LLC
Chambersburg PA
CBHW041223040426

42443CB00002B/72

* 9 7 8 0 9 9 0 8 2 1 7 3 1 *